Blue Banner Biography

Fergie

PeggySue Wells

Mitchell Lane
PUBLISHERS

P.O. Box 196
Hockessin, Delaware 19707
Visit us on the web: www.mitchelllane.com
Comments? email us: mitchelllane@mitchelllane.com

Printing	1	2	3	4	5	6	7	8	9

Blue Banner Biographies

Library of Congress Cataloging-in-Publication Data
Wells, PeggySue.
  Fergie / by PeggySue Wells.
    p. cm. — (Blue banner biographies)
  Includes bibliographical references, discography (p.   ), filmography (p.   ), and index.
  ISBN 978-1-58415-521-8 (library bound)
  1. Fergie, 1975– —Juvenile literature. 2. Singers—United States—Biography—Juvenile literature.
I. Title.
  ML3930.F37W45 2008
  782.42164092--dc22
  [B]
                                                                                    2007019801

ABOUT THE AUTHOR: PeggySue Wells is the author of many books, including *What To Do When You Don't Know What To Say*, and *What To Do When You Don't Want To Go To Church*. She has written hundreds of articles that have appeared nationally in newspapers and magazines, including *Focus on the Family Magazine*, *In Touch Magazine*, and *Homecoming Magazine*. The developer and host of the Kids Track for the national Gaither Praise Gathering, she has written curriculum and conducted classes and workshops at schools, retreats, and conferences. She is the button-popping proud mother of seven children. Learn more about PeggySue at her web site, PeggySueWells.com.

PHOTO CREDITS: Cover—Henry McGee/Globe Photos, Inc. pp. 4, 7—Disney/Kids Incorporated; p. 10—Brenda Chase/Getty Images; p 13—Kevin Winter/DCP/Getty Images; pp. 15, 25—Peter Kramer/Getty Images; p. 20—Rob Loud/Getty Images; p. 23—Frederick M. Brown/Getty Images; p. 26—Chris Hondros/Getty Images; p. 27—Amanda Edwards/Getty Images;

PUBLISHER'S NOTE: The following story has been thoroughly researched, and to the best of our knowledge represents a true story. While every possible effort has been made to ensure accuracy, the publisher will not assume liability for damages caused by inaccuracies in the data, and makes no warranty on the accuracy of the information contained herein. This story has not been authorized or endorsed by Stacy Ferguson.

Blue Banner Biography

Stacy Ann Ferguson, better known by her stage name Fergie, began her career as a child actor on the popular television show Kids Incorporated. *Born in Southern California, she had a strict Catholic upbringing. Stacy was the all-American girl who knew at age seven that she wanted to be an entertainer and have her own solo album.*

She Made It

*I*n front of the mirror in her Southern California home, nine-year-old Stacy Ferguson practiced choreographed moves for the taping of *Kids Incorporated*. Her long blond curls falling over her shoulders, Stacy sang the spirited children's television theme song lyrics, "Looks like we made it."

Even as a child, Stacy wanted to entertain. "She was always dancing for everyone," said her mom, Terri Jackson, in an interview with *Rolling Stone*. "We'd go to the county fair and she wasn't in the shows or anything, but she'd just hop up on a makeshift stage and sing and dance."

Prior to becoming a regular on the popular series *Kids Incorporated*, Stacy auditioned for many parts, always hopeful that this time she'd make it. She was the voice of character Sally Brown in the 1984 Charlie Brown special, *It's Flashbeagle, Charlie Brown*, and in the 1985 *Snoopy's Getting Married, Charlie Brown*.

When she was eight, Stacy landed a spot on Nickelodeon's *Kids Incorporated*. As it did for Martika, Jennifer Love Hewitt, and Rahsaan Patterson, *Kids*

Incorporated launched Stacy's career. Her first name doubled as her character name. As "Stacy," a blond, blue-eyed, well-scrubbed girl, Stacy appeared in over 100 of the 150 shows from September 1984 to February 1994. She starred in more first-run episodes than any other cast member and was the only series regular to progress from being the littlest and youngest to the biggest and eldest performer on the team.

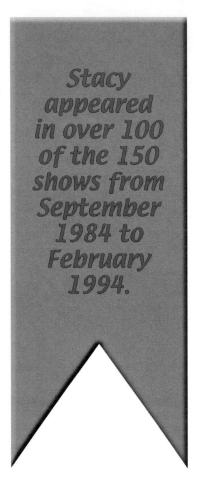

Stacy appeared in over 100 of the 150 shows from September 1984 to February 1994.

Consisting of five actors and five dancers, *Kids Incorporated* was a musical sitcom (situation comedy) about a group of children and teenagers who performed in their own rock group. Band members dealt with real-life issues ranging from divorce to violence to schoolyard crushes while performing regularly at a local soda shop, the P*lace. *Kids Incorporated* was a visual feast of costumes and color, design and dance, movement and music. Stacy acted, danced, and sang.

Canceled in 1985, the show was given a second chance when Disney bought the rights. The program ran on the Disney Channel from November 1986 until February 1994. Disney continued to air reruns until 1996.

During her growing-up years, Stacy and her friends would cruise to the beach listening to Guns N' Roses. Some of her chola friends (tough Mexican girls known for wearing dark lipstick and big hair) preferred cruising to oldies. "I

From 1983 to 1989, Stacy (second from right) starred on Kids Incorporated. *The program won numerous Young Artist Awards and was popular with kids who were teens in the 1980s.*

used to do my hair and clothes in exactly the same way," she said in an MTV interview. "I was always kind of eclectic in my tastes."

Another early experience that influenced her singing style was a concert she attended when she was six. "I saw Tina Turner, second row, with my dad. She pointed at me. That was big," Stacy said. "I love how she was energetic and raw. Those early impressions tell you how things are supposed to be. I've taken a lot of that with me."

From *Kids Incorporated*, Stacy gained experience singing and dancing onstage with a mic. The music and fashion styles of Stacy's chola girlfriends and Tina Turner's singing style were elements Stacy would take with her as she molded her career.

Going Crazy

Born on March 27, 1975, in Whittier, California, Stacy Ann Ferguson grew up in nearby Hacienda Heights. She attended Glen A. Wilson High School. Stacy's parents, Terri Gore and Patrick Ferguson, who were both teachers, and her younger sister, Dana, encouraged Stacy's dreams of a career in entertainment.

When she was seven, Stacy knew what she wanted. "I was going to have an album and that was it. I told my mom that's what I was going to do. She said, 'Okay. As long as you get good grades.' " Even with her busy work schedule, Stacy was a straight-A student.

"In junior high I was fascinated by gangsta rap," she told *Rolling Stone.* "I was suburban, yet I had glimpses [of gangsta life] from where I lived. I'm hearing all the stories about what was going on in East L.A. and South Central, looking at it from the outside. I think I come from a whole generation of that. That's why a lot of people can relate with me, because they lived that, too."

As a teenager, Stacy transitioned from playing a singer on television to being a singer when she fronted her own pop group, Wild Orchid. The female trio included fellow *Kids Incorporated* stars Renee Sandstrom and Stefanie Ridel. Wild Orchid released two albums.

Premiering October 31, 1998, Wild Orchid hosted a children's reality show called *Great Pretenders*. On the show, teenagers lip-synced their favorite songs. The performances were judged by the studio audience. The singer with the most votes was inducted as the Great Pretender. The show last aired in September 2002.

While she was a member of Wild Orchid, Stacy was a model for Bongo and Guess. She was making her dreams reality—until RCA put on the brakes. The recording label declined to release the band's third album.

RCA's decision triggered an emotional crisis for Stacy. She left Wild Orchid and, adrift, she turned to drugs. She was quickly addicted.

"It started on the weekends and graduated to all the time," she said. "Me and my girlfriends would get ready, go out to the club, come home, change into my faux-fur coats and my sunglasses and rent a limo—spending all my child-actor money—and go to the club Garage that would start at 6:00 AM and dance till 12. Then I graduated to crystal. . . . It became less of a fun thing and more of a habit."

She told a Glasgow newspaper, "I started doing Ecstasy. Then I got addicted to crystal methamphetamine. My weight dropped to ninety pounds. Finally, I started going crazy."

> RCA put on the brakes. The recording label declined to release the band's third album.

In her mid-teens, Stacy formed and fronted her own band, Wild Orchid, with Renee Ilene Sandstrom (right) and Stefanie Ridel (left), who were also from Kids Incorporated. Mostly self-written, their self-titled debut album sold nearly a million units worldwide.

The change alarmed those around her. "I noticed her losing a lot of weight," her mother said. "[At first] I was like, 'Wow. Good for you. Wish I could do that.' And then it started to be more and more, and it was, 'Are you okay?' "

Stacy's addiction led to paranoia, and her weight dropped to dangerously low levels. One night Stacy realized she was in trouble. Driving, she pulled to the side of the road and wrote lyrics for a song titled "Losing My Ground":

> *I woke up short of breath*
> > *but I've still got a long day ahead of me*
> *I don't know what day it is*
> > *but tell me 'cause I gotta know who to be*
> *Is this me up in the mirror?*

The words echoed the confusion and loneliness Stacy experienced as a result of her drug use. She brought the lyrics to the girls in Wild Orchid, who realized their friend needed help. Her band members took action and arranged an intervention. They brought together people who were close to Stacy to offer support for recovery.

"So I lied," Stacy said. "I came up with the quickest explanation I could: bulimia. Everyone around me knew, and I didn't care. I just didn't want them to ask me questions."

Denying the problem made things worse. "I became more and more isolated, and it became more and more dark," Stacy described. "One day I started not knowing who I was, and there was this little voice inside of me—God or my conscience—and I had a conversation with me: 'Either go this way or that way. Which road do you wanna choose?' "

Over the telephone she admitted to her mom, "I'm in trouble, and I need to get out of this place."

At age twenty-five, Stacy moved in with her mother and began therapy. "I came clean with everybody and started my life over," she said. Untangling herself from drugs required hard work and counseling. Finally clean, Stacy got a ring in her right eyebrow. Daily she wanted to remind herself how difficult the road to freedom had been.

She has learned to talk about her feelings instead of trying to deal with them through drugs.

Later, in 2006, Stacy talked about her addiction with *Time* magazine. "It was the hardest boyfriend I ever had to break up with," she said. "It's the drug that's addicting. But it's why you start doing it in the first place that's interesting. A lot of it was being a child actor; I learned to suppress feelings." As a young actress, Stacy learned to look as if everything were fine on the outside, even when she was falling apart emotionally.

"In *Kids Incorporated*, I'm in the studio at eight years old, behind a microphone, learning the techniques," she described. "I was a little adult. I had to be professional on the set—you can't break out into a tantrum, so I learned. I always wanted to appease and put on a strong face and not let anyone know if there was something bothering me."

She has learned to talk about her feelings instead of trying to deal with them through drugs. Years later, she reported that she still uses therapy as a lifeline.

Stacy overcame drug addiction and rebuilt her career as a singer, songwriter, and performer. "You'll stop doing drugs, and you'll say I know where that goes and I never want to go there again." In "A Letter to Me at 17," for Seventeen magazine, she said, "Everyday you'll be grateful for how blessed your life is. You know you're not perfect and you allow yourself to make mistakes. Sometimes you'll make a few too many. But don't worry, you'll always come back to your roots."

Black Eyed Peas

Stacy's drug addiction not only hurt her body, mind, career, and relationships, it also depleted her finances. "The trust fund of money I'd made as a child actor, I had to use that to pay off all my credit card debts. Tens of thousands of dollars," she told *Rolling Stone*. "I started living off of unemployment . . . , seeing if there were any writers I could work with, any home studios I could get into."

Working at various Los Angeles venues as a dance floor regular and backup singer, Stacy met Will.i.am of the Black Eyes Peas. The band was formed in 1988 as Atban Klann, when William Adams (now Will.i.am) and Allan Pineda Lindo (now Apl.de.ap) rapped and performed around Los Angeles. In 1995, the group re-formed as the Black Eyed Peas and added Taboo Nawasha (Jaime Gomez). With their third recording project nearly complete, the Peas were looking for a female voice for *Elephunk*.

"I said, 'I need a girl on this who sings hard,' " Will.i.am told *Rolling Stone*, " 'that isn't a girly girl but is raw. Not raw like ghetto, but like some Pat Benatar.' " A friend suggested Stacy.

Since their 2003 breakout album, Black Eyed Peas band members (from left to right) Apl.de.ap, Stacy (Fergie), Taboo, and Will.i.am have received international fame for their pop and dance style of hip-hop music. Worldwide the Black Eyed Peas have sold an estimated 20 million albums and singles.

In the recording studio, Stacy sang the female lead, replacing background singer Kim Hill, who had left the Black Eyed Peas in 2000. The Peas were impressed. "We'd be in the studio till the wee hours," she said, "and we'd go to clubs and go out dancing, and we started becoming this family."

After recording five songs, in 2003 Stacy was invited to become a permanent member.

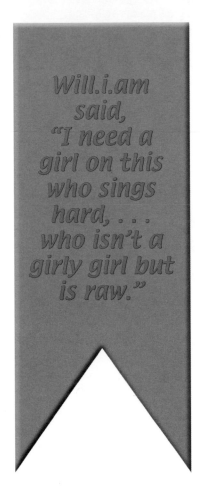

Will.i.am said, "I need a girl on this who sings hard, . . . who isn't a girly girl but is raw."

Black-eyed peas are a traditional soul food. The group chose the name of the food to represent their music for the soul. When the alternative rap group started out, they shunned gangsta rap's aggression and materialism in favor of socially conscious lyrics. Joining Black Eyes Peas members Will.i.am, Apl.de.ap, and Taboo, Stacy Ferguson took the stage name Fergie, or Fergie Ferg, to better match the group's ghetto-funk style.

"Everyone has their different look," she said. "Will's got his knickers and crazy socks, and Taboo has his kung fu wear. I have to think of words to put my style into. I would say kind of urban gypsy, because I collect things, accessories from all over the world and that is definitely what, for me, helps make an outfit my own."

With Stacy, the Black Eyed Peas transitioned from underground success to mainstream popularity. A Black Eyed Peas performance is known for its break dancing. "They're the best dancers on the planet," Stacy said of her fellow band members. "So for me, I was kind of timid at first. And little by little, I would work my way in to figure out where I fit in on the stage."

The third album for the Black Eyed Peas, *Elephunk*, was the first release that included Stacy. Propelled by the single "Where Is the Love," which featured Justin Timberlake, *Elephunk* sold eight million copies worldwide. The recording earned four Grammy nominations and one Grammy Award.

After their global tour, the Black Eyed Peas recorded the even bigger *Monkey Business* and became the world's most popular hip-hop group. Their summer schedule included performing their unique blend of hip and corniness for 150,000 in Moscow's Red Square.

Inspired by the success of the Black Eyed Peas, Stacy turned her attention to the solo project she had dreamed of when she was seven.

With Stacy, the Black Eyed Peas transitioned from underground success to mainstream popularity.

Tiara for the Dutchess

Stacy continued to record and tour with the Black Eyed Peas while completing her first solo project, *The Dutchess*. Most of *The Dutchess* was recorded in a tour-bus studio. As executive producer for Stacy's album, Will.i.am collaborated with Stacy on her arrangements. He preferred to leave the stage after a live performance and go right to work on songs while the energy of the crowd was still inspiring.

During a two-month vacation from touring, the group rented a house with a studio in Malibu, California. The relaxing estate came complete with horses. "It's very different than tour life," Stacy shared. "It's serene and peaceful, and I could be alone and get into those intimate feelings I wanted to express on the record." In this quiet setting, Stacy reworked "Losing My Ground" and included it on *The Dutchess*.

When *The Dutchess* was nearly complete, Stacy received good news about her first solo single, "London Bridge." "I was in California at Josh's house," she recalled in an interview with *Rolling Stone*. "I looked at my Sidekick and it says, 'You're #1 on Billboard Hot 100.' Going Number One on Billboard has been a dream for so long. I started crying, bawling really. It was a happy cry but . . . I felt like I was seven again. I started going over my life, all the ups and downs, everything that I've worked for. And finally this. It's risiculous."

Stacy includes made-up words in her songs. "When something is so, so sick, it's risiculous. It's sick and ridiculous. Risiculous." She told *Rolling Stone*, "I'm not that categorizable, if that's a word. But it is in my dictionary."

She also said, "I love imitating instruments. Sometimes you can't understand what I'm saying because I'm going for an instrumental sound. It would ruin the sound if I pronunciated correctly."

Released in September 2006, *The Dutchess* was a play on names, as Stacy's surname and nickname are the same as Sarah Ferguson's, the Duchess of York. The multiplatinum album includes the hit songs "London Bridge," "Glamorous," and "Fergalicious."

"I looked at my Sidekick and it says, 'You're #1 on Billboard Hot 100.'"

It also includes "Big Girls Don't Cry," which "was written before I was in the Black Eyed Peas," Stacy told *AIM*. "It's all about independence. 'All That I've Got' is about loving someone for inner beauty. All of my songs on *The Dutchess* are true stories." Lyrics in "Glamorous" refer to Stacy's normal life. "It's about the dichotomy of the way I grew up and the life I'm living now," she said. "I'm still the same girl who isn't moved out of mom's yet. I get to stay at these lavish hotels

Stacy wore a black Gucci gown to the release party for The Dutchess. *"This dress I bought for [Josh Duhamel's] sister's wedding, so I wore it again," she said. "Yes, I wear things again. I like it. I feel comfortable in it." For the special occasion, Will.i.am presented Stacy with a diamond necklace and a stunning tiara.*

but I still go directly from the airport to Jack-in-the-Box or Taco Bell or Del Taco because they are my comfort foods."

On *MTV News*, Stacy talked about the "London Bridge" video, shot in London. "We got to use the whole cheeky London-type thing, playing with the British guards," she said. "But at the same time, we were playing with the '60s London feel, with the Brigitte Bardot bouffant hair, and mixing that up with the chola style. It's kind of a weird fusion, and it somehow just all works together."

Playing off the album's royal name, Stacy designed an outfit for her video from her family's Scottish crest and tartan. She wore a tiara cocked to one side of her head.

The launch party for Stacy's solo project was a royal affair at a Manhattan hot spot. According to *MTV News*, Will.i.am took the stage and invited Stacy to join him. "In the year 2002, I had the pleasure of meeting Fergie Ferg and we all took sacrifices," Will.i.am said. "She took a sacrifice by putting her solo career aside and doing the Black Eyed Peas. And we made the sacrifice by not knowing where we were going to go. But we went into it with open hearts and open minds. And here we are three and a half years later releasing Fergie's solo album. We've recorded all over the world — Australia, Beijing, London, Paris, Canada, America, Mexico. And this project has been so important to me to stand alongside Fergie Ferg and record in the studio, and out of appreciation for her trusting me, I've got something I want to give to her."

He draped a large diamond necklace on Stacy's neck and crowned her with a diamond tiara. "A duchess wouldn't be complete without a proper crown," he said.

Stacy thanked Will.i.am for "believing in me when I was living at my mom's and just really understanding that girl that was in suburbia and seeing something that was in her."

"We've recorded all over the world — Australia, Beijing, London, Paris, Canada, America, Mexico."

CHAPTER
5

Silver Screen

*S*tacy continued to mix music with acting. On numerous television guest spots, she and the Black Eyed Peas would appear as themselves. In 2004, the band played on the series *Las Vegas* in an episode titled "Montecito Lancers." There, Stacy met and began dating American actor and series regular Josh Duhamel.

Stacy appeared in *Poseidon*, the 2006 big-budget remake of the 1972 film *The Poseidon Adventure*. "I'm a singer on the ship," she said, "so the role is not really a stretch." Stacy sang a ballad she cowrote with Will.i.am and drummer Keith Harris, titled "I Won't Let You Fall." "It's very nineties Mariah [Carey] or Whitney [Houston]," she described. "It goes with the theme of the movie and the whole diva character — very larger than life. I definitely die. You don't see me die, but I do. It's short and sweet. I'm out!"

Released in 2007, *Grindhouse*, rated R, was a double feature. Two thrillers, *Death Proof* and the zombie movie *Planet Terror*, are played as one long film. Stacy had a minor role as Tammy Visan in *Planet Terror*, written and directed by Robert Rodriguez.

Stacy attended the Hollywood premiere of Poseidon. Acting as a singer on the Warner Brothers action adventure film, Stacy performed a song she cowrote for the movie and "Auld Lang Syne" for the opulent cruise ship guests. They were unaware that a rogue wave was bearing down on them, about to turn their New Year's holiday upside down.

With all her success, Stacy could afford to buy big-name bags. "I've just started buying expensive bags like the Fendi B bag and a brand-new big Burberry with a gold chain," she said in an *AIM* interview. "I wouldn't buy things like that before because it wasn't realistic."

A fashion icon, Stacy combined her unique style with her love for handbags, designing two collections for Kipling North America. Featuring unique designs and silhouettes, the handbags would launch in fall 2007 through summer 2008.

"As with every project that I'm involved with, I plan to put all of my heart and creativity into this one, and I'm thrilled to work with such an amazing brand," said Stacy. "I look forward to putting my personal touch on each and every design in my . . . collections."

Stacy is also involved with the Black Eyed Peas' global Peapod Foundation. "The Black Eyes Peas did this for years before I was in the band," she said. "But I'm always a sucker for a good cause. I hope we can be of help to people who are in need right now."

Earlier, playing on Los Angeles stages, the Black Eyed Peas would invite fellow musicians on stage to jam. Afterward, they collected the cans and bottles and put the earnings toward charity. As the band catapulted from humble beginnings to international phenomenon, the size of their benefit concerts and money raised for their foundation multiplied.

> "I look forward to putting my personal touch on each and every design in my . . . collections."

Stacy performs "London Bridge" for Dick Clark's New Year's Rockin' Eve 2007. The song was her first chart topper, followed by "Fergalicious" and "Glamorous." "London Bridge" climbed fast, reaching the top in its second chart week. The Dutchess went platinum in the United States and Japan.

Stacy and the Black Eyed Peas won diverse and international fans through their energetic hip-hop, loose rhyme schemes, and funkafied vibe. Whether singing on tour or walking the red carpet, Stacy's unique blend of clothing and international accessories has gained her a reputation as a fashion icon.

Responding to the Southeast Asian tsunami of 2004, the Black Eyed Peas and friends performed at the first Peapod Foundation benefit concert, raising vital dollars for tsunami relief. In 2006, the second annual event at Hollywood's Henry Fonda Theater brought together music legends of the past, present, and future to raise awareness and funds for the Peapod Foundation's children's charities.

In May of that year, Stacy traveled with the group on their first international charitable endeavor with a free concert for more than 70,000 people living in rural South

The Black Eyed Peas lent their support to worthy causes through free concerts, toy drives, and volunteer projects. During the week of the Grammy Awards, Stacy took the stage with her band mates and numerous fellow entertainers for the Peapod Concert Benefit for Children's Charities.

Africa. Performing alongside acclaimed South African artists and dancers, the Black Eyed Peas spotlighted the plight of children and vowed to combat global issues affecting orphaned, foster, and impoverished children. The event raised funds for South Africa's Adopt-A-School Program.

The foundation also plans to establish arts and recording academies around the world for underprivileged children — beginning with one in the band's own backyard. Stacy and the Black Eyed Peas grew up in the Los Angeles area, which, according to the foundation's web site, "is home to over 30,000 foster children alone who are at the greatest risk of being abused, traumatized, homeless, poor; and later in life, jobless and incarcerated."

All four band members know the sting of poverty and credit music for moving them into a better life. Their third annual benefit, held in 2007 at Avalon in Hollywood, provided funds to launch a state-of-the-art music educational and recording facility that would serve these children.

" 'Yo, I'm having a dance-off!' 'With who?' 'With myself!' She looks in the mirror and goes at it."

An international sensation, Stacy works out every day and has meals delivered by a diet service so that she doesn't have to count calories. In 2007, she walked the red carpet to receive a Grammy Award for the year's Best Pop Performance by a Group with Vocals for their song "My Humps." As she had sung for the theme song of *Kids Incorporated*, Stacy has definitely made it.

And she still performs for the mirror. In a *Rolling Stone* article, Taboo said, "She'll dance in the hotel by herself. I'll call her up and she'll say, 'Yo, I'm having a dance-off!' 'With who?' 'With myself!' She looks in the mirror and goes at it."

CHRONOLOGY

1975   Stacy Ann Ferguson is born in Whittier, California, on March 27.

1984- 1985

Stacy is the voice of Sally Brown for the Charlie Brown specials, *It's Flashbeagle, Charlie Brown* and *Snoopy's Getting Married, Charlie Brown*.

1984   Stacy lands the role of "Stacy" on the television series *Kids Incorporated*.

1993   She graduates from Glen A. Wilson High School.

1990s   Atban Klann, with future Black Eyed Peas band members, forms in Los Angeles.

1991   Stacy becomes one of the female trio *Wild Orchid*.

1995   Taboo joins Atban Klann, which is renamed Black Eyed Peas.

1998   Black Eyed Peas release their first album, *Behind the Front*.

1998   Wild Orchid hosts *Great Pretenders*, a reality show for children.

2000   Black Eyed Peas release second album, *Bridging the Gap*. Stacy begins therapy to address her drug addiction.

2003   Stacy joins the Black Eyes Peas and becomes known as Fergie. They release *Elephunk*, their third album, and go on a world tour.

2004   Fergie is chosen by *People* magazine as one of the world's most beautiful people.

2005   The Black Eyed Peas release their fourth album, *Monkey Business*. Fergie is cast as Stevie Wayne in John Carpenter's *The Fog*. Later she backs out over creative differences. She has a guest role on the *Rocket Power* special, Reggie's *Big Beach Break*, on Nickelodeon. She voices a fictitious pop music star named Shaffika. The Peapod Foundation holds a benefit concert to aid victims of the tsunami in Indonesia.

2006   Fergie and the Black Eyes Peas are nominated for four Grammy Awards. They take home one Grammy for the year's best pop performance by a group with vocals for their song "My Humps." Fergie appears in a minor role in *Poseidon*. The Peapod Foundation hosts a star-studded benefit concert for children's charities around the world. It also hosts a free Black Eyed Peas concert in Johannesburg, South Africa, to raise awareness of global issues that affect children. Fergie releases *The Dutchess*.

2007   Fergie appears in the feature film *Grindhouse*. The Peapod Foundation hosts their third annual benefit concert, auctioning speakers signed by stars including the Black Eyed Peas.

FILMOGRAPHY

2007	*Life on the Road with Mr. and Mrs. Brown* (documentary)
	Grindhouse
2006	*Poseidon*
2005	*Be Cool*
2003	*Rocket Power* (TV, 1 episode)
1998	*Great Pretenders* (TV, with Wild Orchid)
1997	*Goode Behavior* (TV, 1 episode)
	An American Vampire Story
1995	*California Dreams* (TV, 1 episode)
1987	*Monster in the Closet*
1986	*Mr. Belvedere* (TV, 1 episode)
1985	*Snoopy's Getting Married, Charlie Brown* (voice, Sally Brown)
1984	*It's Flashbeagle, Charlie Brown* (voice, Sally Brown)
1984–1994	
	Kids Incorporated (TV, unknown episodes)

DISCOGRAPHY

Albums

Solo

2006	*The Dutchess*

With Black Eyed Peas

2005	*Monkey Business*
2003	*Elephunk*

With Wild Orchid

1998	*Oxygen*
1997	*Wild Orchid*

Hit Singles with Black Eyed Peas

2003	"Where Is the Love"
2003	"Shut Up"
2004	"Hey, Mama"
2004	"Let's Get It Started"
2005	"Don't Phunk With My Heart"
2005	"Don't Lie"
2005	"My Humps"

Hit Solo Singles

2006	"London Bridge"
2006	"Fergalicious"
2007	"Glamorous"

FURTHER READING

Books

If you enjoyed this biography of Fergie, you might also like to read these other hip-hop and rock biographies from Mitchell Lane Publishers:

Beyoncé
Christina Aguilera
Gwen Stefani
Justin Timberlake
Mariah Carey
Mary J. Blige
Shakira

Works Consulted

AOL Music. "Fergie AIM Interview." http://music.aol.com/artists/aim-celebrity-interview/fergie-page-1

Baltin, Steve. "Up in It: Fergie Sets Sail." *Rolling Stone*, November 20, 2005. http://www.rollingstone.com/artists/crosbystillsandnash/articles/story/8898188/up_in_it

"Fab Flash: Fergie Signs Handbag Deal with Kipling." FABSUGAR, March 26, 2007. http://fabsugar.com/185184

"Fergie." TV.com. www.tv.com/fergie/person/274877/summary.html

Hasty, Katie. "Fergie Gets 'Glamorous' Atop Hot 100." *Billboard.com*, March 15, 2007. http://www.billboard.com/bbcom/news/article_display.jsp?vnu_content_id=1003558736

Touré. "Fergie Dances With Herself." *Rolling Stone*, October 3, 2006. http://www.rollingstone.com/news/coverstory/fergie_dances_with_herself

Vineyard, Jennifer. With additional reporting by Simi Nahil and Corey Moss. "Fergie Gets Rough and Regal In First Video From Solo LP." *VH1.com News*, August 12, 2006. http://www.vh1.com/news/articles/1536116/20060711/black_eyed_peas.jhtml

Weinstein, Farrah. "Fergie Gets Blinged Out, Overwhelmed at *Dutchess* Release Party." *MTV News*, September 22, 2006. http://www.mtv.com/news/articles/1541572/20060922/fergie__4_.jhtml?headlines=true

Ferguson, Stacy. "A Letter to Me at 17." *Seventeen*, June 2007, p. 104.

Web Sites

The Official Black Eyed Peas Website: www.blackeyedpeas.com
The Official Fergie Website: www.fergie.com
The Peapod Foundation: www.peapodfoundation.org/

INDEX